MW00388695

LOSE CONTROL

The Way to Find Your Soul

LEADER GUIDE

MARY SHANNON HOFFPAUIR

Jenny Youngman, contributor

Abingdon Women | Nashville

Lose Control Leader Guide
The Way to Find Your Soul

ISBN-13: 978-1-7910-0437-8

20 21 22 23 24 25 26 27 28 29 — 10 9 8 7 6 5 4 3 2 1
MANUFACTURED IN THE UNITED STATES OF AMERICA

Contents

About the Author

Mary Shannon is a powerful and seasoned Bible teacher, author, and speaker whose great love for Jesus and Scripture inspires her audiences to "get their face in the Book!" Her background is rich with a spiritual upbringing rooted solidly in the Bible. But as a self-professed recovering perfectionist, she was bound by performance-based theology much of her Christian life, believing God's affection and approval were contingent on toeing the line of legalism—on measuring up. Most comfortable in a ball cap and ripped jeans, Mary Shannon is a gifted storyteller with a sassy sense of humor and a fresh transparency about the messiness of life: a recipe providing her with fresh insight and ample illustrations that are sure to make you laugh and cry as she brings the Bible to life for the ordinary person. After teaching the Bible in the classroom for many years, she began to teach women in her community; and today she leads three large community women's Bible study groups in the Phoenix metropolitan area (200–300 women each), as well as teaches across the nation as a featured speaker with the Aspire Women's Events. The loves of her life are her daughter, Hillary, and her late son, Zach (1994–2020).

Follow Mary Shannon:

 @ itsmaryshannon

 @ itsmaryshannon

Video messages/blog   itsmaryshannon.com
(check here also for event dates and booking information)

Introduction

The Book of First Samuel is an epic story about a fight for control. It is the saga of Saul and David, Israel's first two kings, and it has much to teach us about the battle for control in our own lives. Many of us say that God is in control while living our lives as if we're the ones who have to hold it all together. It's like walking around with a cup of hot coffee, afraid it will spill with one wrong move. And when it does, making a mess, we realize what little control we actually have and how dependent on God we are.

My own experience of what that is like was the impetus for me writing this study. But I never could have imagined that before the writing process was over, I would find myself losing control once again when my beloved son, Zachary, died suddenly and unexpectedly. I had no idea how much I would lean into and even learn from the very principles I wrote about in this study. Yet I am finding more than ever that God's promises are true and His presence is what sustains me—even in the darkest caves and longest nights I have ever experienced.

My prayer for the women in your group as they journey through First Samuel is that they would discover that no plan or purpose of God can be thwarted by human beings or any circumstance. I pray they will be able to see God's purposes in their lives, no matter what path they find themselves walking. And I pray they can begin to let go of their attempts to orchestrate the events of their lives to a desired end and, instead, to risk losing control in order to discover just how much they can trust our loving, sovereign God.

About the Participant Workbook

Before the first session, you will want to distribute copies of the *Lose Control* participant workbook to the members of your group. Be sure to communicate that they are to complete the first week of readings *before* your first group session. For each week, there are five readings or lessons that combine study of Scripture with personal reflection and application. On average, each lesson can be completed in about twenty to thirty minutes. Completing these readings each week will prepare the women for the discussion and activities of the group session.

About This Leader Guide

As you gather each week with the members of your group, you will have the opportunity to watch a video, discuss and respond to what you're learning, and pray together. You will need access to a television and DVD player with working remotes, or, if you're downloading the video sessions from online, a computer with a screen large enough for the group to watch together. (Streaming video files are available at www.Cokesbury.com, or you may access the video for this study and other Abingdon Women studies on AmplifyMedia.com through an individual or church membership.)

Creating a warm and inviting atmosphere will help make the women feel welcome. Although optional, you might consider providing snacks and drinks or coffee for your first meeting and inviting group members to rotate in bringing refreshments each week.

This Leader Guide and the video lessons will be your primary tools for leading each group session. In this Leader Guide you will find outlines for six group sessions, each formatted for either a 60-minute or 90-minute group session:

60-Minute Format

Leader Prep (Before the Session)

Welcome and Opening Prayer	2 minutes
Icebreaker	3 minutes
Video	25–30 minutes
Group Discussion	20 minutes
Closing Prayer	3–5 minutes

90-Minute Format

Leader Prep (Before the Session)

Welcome and Opening Prayer	2 minutes
Icebreaker	3 minutes
Video	25–30 minutes

Group Discussion	35 minutes
Deeper Conversation	15 minutes
Closing Prayer	5 minutes

As you can see, the 90-minute format is identical to the 60-minute format but has more time for group discussion, plus a Deeper Conversation exercise for small groups. Feel free to adapt or modify either of these formats, as well as the individual segments and activities, in any way to meet the specific needs and preferences of your group.

Here is a brief overview of the elements included in both formats:

Leader Prep (Before the Session)

For your preparation prior to the group session, this section provides an overview of the week's biblical story and theme, key Scriptures, and a list of materials and equipment needed. Be sure to review this section, as well as read through the *entire* session outline, before your group time in order to plan and prepare. You will not have enough time to discuss every question provided in this Leader Guide, so choose the ones you think will best address your group's needs. If you choose, you also may find it helpful to watch the video lesson in advance.

Welcome and Opening Prayer (2 minutes)

Create a warm, welcoming environment as the women are gathering before the session begins. Consider lighting one or more candles, providing coffee or other refreshments, and/or playing worship music. (Bring an iPod, smartphone, or tablet and a portable speaker if desired.) Be sure to provide nametags if the women do not know one another or you have new participants in your group. Then, when you are ready to begin, open the group in prayer before you begin your time.

You also may find it helpful to read aloud the week's Overview found in the Leader Prep section if not all group members have completed their homework.

Icebreaker (3 minutes)

Use the icebreaker to briefly engage the women in the topic while helping them feel comfortable with one another.

Video (25–30 minutes)

Next, watch the week's video segment together. Be sure to direct participants to the Video Viewer Guide in the participant workbook, which they may complete as they watch the video. (Answers are provided on page 63 of this guide and page 202 in the participant workbook.)

Group Discussion (20–35 minutes, depending on session length)

After watching the video, choose from the questions provided to facilitate group discussion. Questions are provided for both the video segment and the participant workbook material. For the Participant Workbook Discussion Questions, you may choose to read aloud the discussion points, which are excerpted from the participant workbook, or express them in your own words; then use one or more of the questions that follow to guide your conversation.

Note that more material is provided than you will have time to include. Before the session, select what you want to cover, putting a check mark beside it in your book. Reflect on each question and make some notes in the margins to share during your discussion time. Page references are provided for those questions that relate to specific questions or activities in the participant workbook. For these questions, invite group members to turn in their workbooks to the pages indicated. Participants will need Bibles in order to look up various supplementary Scripture.

Depending on the number of women in your group and the level of their participation, you may not have time to cover everything you have selected, and that is okay. Rather than attempting to bulldoze through the material, follow the Spirit's leadership and be open to where the Spirit takes the conversation. Remember, your role is not to have all the answers but to encourage discussion and sharing.

Deeper Conversation (15 minutes)

If your group meets for 90 minutes, use this section for deeper sharing in small groups, dividing into groups of two or three if necessary. This is a time for women to share more intimately and build stronger connections with one another. (Encourage the women to break into different groups each week.) Give a two-minute warning before time is up so the groups can wrap up their discussions.

Closing Prayer (3–5 minutes, depending on session length)

Close by leading the group in prayer. If you'd like, invite the women to briefly name prayer requests. To get things started, you might share a personal request of your own. As women share their requests, model for the group by writing each request in your participant workbook, indicating that you will remember to pray for them during the week.

As the study progresses, you might encourage members to participate in the Closing Prayer by praying out loud for one another and the requests given. Ask the women to volunteer to pray for specific requests, or have each woman pray for the woman on her right or left. Make sure nametags are visible so that group members do not feel awkward if they do not remember someone's name.

Before You Begin

Leading a group of women through a Bible study on control is not for the faint of heart. But here's what I know: when our circumstances and our faith are shaken, that is when we can finally let go of our exhausted and futile attempts to pretend that we have it all together. That is when we realize that we don't have control, and never did. That is when we learn to trust God as never before and truly surrender. And in the process of surrendering, we find our soul, which is tethered to our unshakable, unfailing God.

I am grateful for your willingness to lead a group of women on this journey. Thank you for sacrificing your time and energy to study, prepare, and pray for God to work. Be open to how the Spirit leads, and don't worry when your time together goes differently than you planned. Remember, God is *always* working. Follow His lead, and He will do more than you could ask or imagine (Ephesians 3:20). Surrender control, and watch Him work—in their lives and in yours.

Mary Shannon

Leader Helps

Preparing for the Sessions

- Decide whether you will use the 60-minute or 90-minute format option. Be sure to communicate dates and times to participants in advance.
- Distribute participant workbooks to all members at least one week before your first session and instruct them to complete the first week's readings. If you have the phone numbers or email addresses of your group members, send out a reminder and a welcome.
- Check out your meeting space before each group session. Make sure the room is ready. Do you have enough chairs? Do you have the equipment and supplies you need? (See the list of materials needed in each session outline.)
- Pray for your group and each group member by name. Ask God to work in the life of every woman who participates.
- Read and complete the week's readings in the participant workbook and review the session outline in the Leader Guide. Select the discussion points and questions you want to cover and make some notes in the margins to share in your discussion time.

Leading the Sessions

- Personally welcome and greet each woman as she arrives. You might want to have a signup list for the women to record their names and contact information.
- At the start of each session, ask the women to turn off or silence their cell phones.

- Always start on time. Honor the time of those who are on time.
- Encourage everyone to participate, but don't put anyone on the spot. Be prepared to offer a personal example or answer if no one else responds at first.
- Communicate the importance of completing the weekly readings and participating in group discussion.
- Facilitate but don't dominate. Remember that if you talk most of the time, group members may tend to listen rather than to engage. Your task is to encourage conversation and keep the discussion moving, not to provide all the answers.
- If someone monopolizes the conversation, kindly thank her for sharing and ask if anyone else has any insights.
- Try not to interrupt, judge, or minimize anyone's comments or input.
- Remember that you are not expected to be the expert. Acknowledge that all of you are on this journey together, with the Holy Spirit as your leader and guide. If issues or questions arise that you don't feel equipped to handle or answer, talk with the pastor or a staff member at your church. It's okay to say, "I don't know."
- Don't rush to fill the silence. If no one speaks right away, it's okay to wait for someone to answer. After a moment, ask, "Would anyone be willing to share?" If no one responds, try asking the question again a different way—or offer a brief response and ask if anyone has anything to add.
- Encourage good discussion, but don't be timid about calling time on a particular question and moving ahead. Part of your responsibility is to keep the group on track. If you decide to spend extra time on a given question or activity, consider skipping or spending less time on another question or activity in order to stay on schedule.
- End on time. If you are running over, give members the opportunity to leave if they need to. Then wrap up as quickly as you can.
- Thank the women for coming and let them know you're looking forward to seeing them next time.
- Be prepared for some women to want to hang out and talk at the end. If you need everyone to leave by a certain time, communicate this at the beginning of the group session. If you are meeting in a church during regularly scheduled activities, be aware of nursery closing times.

Week 1

I Believe God Is in Control

Giving Lip Service
Without
Heart Commitment

(1 SAMUEL 1–6)

Leader Prep (Before the Session)

Overview

Throughout this study, we will explore what it means to let go of the need for control and lean completely into God's promises of presence, faithfulness, and goodness. Even when we can't see God moving, we can be sure that God is in control. And, when we let God be the One in control of our lives, we find our soul.

We'll begin our six-week study of 1 Samuel by diving into the first six chapters. What we find is that the norm of the day was corruption and performance-based religion—one in which Eli the priest and his wayward sons, Hophni and Phinehas, put on a show of love for God but lacked the deeper heart connection.

Key Scriptures

You will seek me and find me, when you seek me with all your heart.
(Jeremiah 29:13)

How long, Lord? Will you forget me forever?
*   How long will you hide your face from me?*
*   (Psalm 13:1 NIV)*

No one has ever seen God, but the one and only Son, who is himself God and is in closest relationship with the Father, has made him known.
(John 1:18 NIV)

For you died, and your life is now hidden with Christ in God.
*   (Colossians 3:3 NIV)*

What You Will Need

- *Lose Control* DVD (or downloads) and a DVD player or computer
- Bible and *Lose Control* participant workbook for reference

- Dry erase board or chart paper and markers (optional)
- Stick-on nametags and markers (optional)
- iPod, smartphone, or tablet and portable speaker (optional)

Session Outline

Welcome and Opening Prayer (2 minutes)

In order to create a warm, welcoming environment as the women are gathering before the session begins, consider lighting one or more candles, providing coffee or other refreshments, and/or playing worship music. (Bring an iPod, smartphone, or tablet and a portable speaker if desired.) Be sure to provide nametags if the women do not know one another or you have new participants in your group. Then, when you are ready to begin, open the group in prayer, or invite someone else to do so.

Icebreaker (3 minutes)

Invite the women to share short responses to the following question:

- On a scale of 1–10 (1 being laid back and 10 being a control freak), how would you rate your need for control? Briefly share a simple example that demonstrates your answer.

Video (25–30 minutes)

Play the Week 1 video segment on the DVD. Invite participants to complete the Video Viewer Guide for Week 1 in the participant workbook as they watch (page 39).

Group Discussion (20–35 minutes, depending on session length)

Note: More material is provided than you will have time to include. Before the session, select what you want to cover.

Video Discussion Questions

- In what ways is culture telling you that you are "not enough"? How has comparison highlighted your feeling of lack?
- Have you ever held out your "love cup" for someone to fill? What did you learn?

- Have you ever walked through a situation that felt without hope, only to see God provide a solution? Explain.

Participant Workbook Discussion Questions

> The only thing that kept Israel in line during the time of the judges was a strong human leader. When a leader was committed to serving the Lord, the people were required to get rid of pagan worship and worship only Yahweh. Yet when that judge died, the people would once again worship pagan gods. I believe the nation of Israel during that time is a prime example of religious reformation, as opposed to spiritual revival.
>
> Religious reformation is a temporary change in behavior due to religious constraints.
>
> Spiritual revival is a permanent change of the heart. (Day 1)

- To you, what is the difference between "religious reformation" and "spiritual revival"?
- How have you learned the difference between religious reformation and spiritual revival in your own journey of faith? Describe how you have experienced each.
- Can you think of a time when you poured out your heart like Hannah did? How did God respond to your cries?

> Eli was used to seeing people live their lives in obedience to a set of rules. They were going through the religious motions with no movement of the heart. Yet lowly Hannah, the exception to the norm, came in to pour out her heart to the Lord. The one who was "raised up" on his high seat or high horse failed to recognize not only true worship in another person, but also his own need for the same. (Day 1)

- Read aloud 1 Samuel 2:12-17 and 22, and describe in your own words the behaviors we see in these sons. (page 15) What did you discover in today's lesson about Eli, Hophni, and Phineas?
- Read aloud 2 Timothy 3:5. In your own words, how would you describe the connection between what 1 Samuel 2:12 says about Hophni and Phinehas and what 2 Timothy 3:5 says about people in the last days? (page 15)

- Read aloud 1 Peter 2:9. What are your thoughts as you compare Eli and his sons to this verse in 1 Peter? What are the privileges and dangers of being a royal priesthood? In what ways might we as Christians or the church have been blockades to the world knowing the goodness of God? (page 16)

Often we forget that we all are called to minister to those around us, and sometimes those in official ministry forget that their position is not one of power or prestige but of service. Even Jesus took the form, or nature, of a servant. (Day 2)

- Read the definition of "minister" on page 19. Are you a minister according to the definition? In what ways do you minister? To whom do you minister? (page 19)
- When have you had the privilege of ministering to someone? Describe that experience.
- Is it easy or difficult to think of yourself as a minister? Why?

God promised that if we seek Him with all of our hearts, we will find Him (Jeremiah 29:13), but doesn't it often seem as if He is purposefully hiding from us? It could be that He has already shown us many things that we are ignoring, and He is patiently waiting for us to address those. (Day 2)

- Read 1 Samuel 3:2-10. Do you believe the description of Eli's eyesight is only literal, or could it also have some spiritual significance? Explain. (page 20)
- What things had Eli overlooked? (page 20)
- When have you felt like God was purposefully hiding from you? Describe the situation.
- Read Psalm 46:10. Why is it important to be still before God?

[The Israelites] had no true shepherd guiding them. They weren't experiencing a deep personal connection with God, and when they prayed, they heard nothing but silence. They were left walking through the motions of life based on ancient teachings, battling whatever came their way with whatever means possible. But this battle had gotten the best of them! This confrontation caused them to run for cover and reevaluate what they were doing. They knew this battle could not be won without the supernatural power of God. This battle was out of their control. It took a great defeat for the people to remember the God of the Exodus, the God of miracles. (Day 3)

- Read 1 Samuel 4:1-4. Have you ever caught yourself living with God as an afterthought, like you've got the Christian-life thing all figured out? What caused you to snap out of it and realize your need for God?
- Have you ever experienced a disconnect between your circumstances and what you believe about God? Explain. (page 26)
- How often do we treat the living God as a graven image to be carried around wherever we need Him? What are some ways that we, like the Israelites, put God in a box? (page 26)

Going through tough times of defeat, suffering, and pain will make us question God. We question His character and motives. When things are bad enough, we even question His existence. (Day 3)

- Have you ever questioned God's existence or character? What were the circumstances?
- Read Psalm 13. What do you think the psalmist was feeling?
- When have you felt stuck in the messy middle between questions and faith? Describe that time. (page 28)

Isn't that how it all started? Wanting to be like God, having knowledge and control. In the Garden, the serpent of old convinced Eve that she could be like God by knowing good and evil. The problem is, differentiating between good and evil is only one aspect of God. Having the knowledge of good and evil without possessing the power to use that knowledge wisely actually leaves us feeling more human than deity. We realize that knowledge does not mean control. Actually, the more knowledgeable I become, the more out of control I often feel. To be honest, sometimes I just want to live with my head in the sand. (Day 4)

- Read Romans 7:8-11. How do these words of Paul affirm the idea that knowledge does not mean control? (page 31)

- Name a situation in your life when you had knowledge but could not control the circumstances.

  _____

  > Yet, God! Don't you love those words? . . . [God] has both knowledge and control—all of which is wrapped in the most beautiful package of grace. He has a plan for you. Release your grip. Leave your broken graven image [of God] on the floor and watch Him work! (Day 4)

- Reflect on your readings from the week. Where do you see "Yet, God" moments in the story unfolding in 1 Samuel?
- What are some "Yet, God" moments in your own life, times when God showed His mercy and grace despite your desire to control the outcome?

  _____

  > I am sure the Israelites came from all over to see this miraculous return of the ark back to them. There must have been great fanfare when they pulled the graven images from the cart one by one, describing what they were and which city they were from. I can just hear the shouting as each city of the Philistines was called out by name, none of which was spared from God's judgment. Yet, then we read something that makes us recoil. Their celebration soon turned to weeping. (Day 5)

- Reread 1 Samuel 6:19-20, also reading Numbers 3:4 for context clues. What happened in these verses? Why did they suffer this fate? (page 34)
- What does this passage reveal about God?
- Read John 1:18. What does this passage tell us about how we can be in relationship with God?

  _____

  > The truth is, we aren't hidden _from_ God, we're hidden _in_ God. We aren't hidden _by_ Christ; we're hidden _with_ Christ (Colossians 3:3). In Jesus, we have been reconciled. He sees us. He delights in us. He wants a relationship with us. In his book _Ragamuffin Gospel_, Brennan Manning explores how God's love is always an open-armed invitation back into authentic relationship, one in which His love sees us as

we are and not as we should be.[1] God never sends us away. I don't believe that sin keeps God from us, but it keeps us from God. And that's good news. (Day 5)

- Read Colossians 3:3. What does it mean to be hidden with Christ in God?
- Have you ever felt like God would send you away? Explain.
- What have you learned this week about God's open-armed invitation?

Deeper Conversation (15 minutes)

Divide into smaller groups of two or three for deeper conversation. If you'd like, before the session, write on a dry erase board or chart paper the question(s) you want the smaller groups to discuss. You could also do this in the form of a handout. Give a two-minute warning before time is up so the groups can wrap up their discussions.

- Think about the title of Week 1: "I Believe God Is in Control: Giving Lip Service Without Heart Commitment." Do you believe God is in control of your situation right now? Explain.
- What does it mean for you personally to go beyond "lip service" and toward "heart commitment"?
- Take another look at the Prayer Prompt questions from Day 5. What is keeping you from a deep connection with your Father right now? Are you assuming things about God that may not be true? (page 38) How have the voices or judgments in your head hampered your ability to receive God's love? Explain.

Closing Prayer (3–5 minutes)

Close the session by taking personal prayer requests from group members and leading the group in prayer. Encourage members to participate by praying out loud for one another and the requests given (as they are comfortable doing so).

---

1 Brennan Manning, *The Ragamuffin Gospel: Good News for the Bedraggled, Beat-Up, and Burnt Out* (Colorado Springs, CO: Multnomah Books, 2005), 46.

Week 2

I've Got This Under Control

Maintaining the Façade

(1 SAMUEL 7–12)

Leader Prep (Before the Session)

Overview

This week we followed the Israelites into a recurring pattern of turning to God and then deciding they'd rather do their own thing apart from God. Samuel becomes their go-to guy—their priest, prophet, and judge. But eventually the people want to be like the other nations and persuade Samuel to ask God to give them a king. After trying to talk them out of it, God relents and Saul comes on the scene.

The people believe this new king will give them the outcome they desired. Samuel tries to tell them that with or without a king, true freedom is found only in God. Ultimately, God is still in control. He is still on the throne. If Saul did not seek the heart of God and lead the people in His ways, the cycle of bondage would continue with or without a king.

Key Scriptures

But the LORD said to Samuel, "Do not consider his appearance or his height, for I have rejected him. The LORD does not look at the things people look at. People look at the outward appearance, but the LORD looks at the heart."

(1 Samuel 16:7 NIV)

²²But the fruit of the Spirit is love, joy, peace, forbearance, kindness, goodness, faithfulness, ²³gentleness and self-control. Against such things there is no law.

(Galatians 5:22-23 NIV)

What You Will Need

- *Lose Control* DVD (or downloads) and a DVD player or computer
- Bible and *Lose Control* participant workbook for reference
- Dry erase board or chart paper and markers (optional)

- Stick-on nametags and markers (optional)
- iPod, smartphone, or tablet and portable speaker (optional)

Session Outline

Welcome and Opening Prayer (2 minutes)

In order to create a warm, welcoming environment as the women are gathering before the session begins, consider lighting one or more candles, providing coffee or other refreshments, and/or playing worship music. (Bring an iPod, smartphone, or tablet and a portable speaker if desired.) Be sure to provide nametags if the women do not know one another or you have new participants in your group. Then, when you are ready to begin, open the group in prayer, or invite someone else to do so.

Icebreaker (3 minutes)

Invite the women to share short responses to the following question:

- What's one thing you can never remember, no matter how hard you try (someone's name, directions to a place, where you put something)?

Video (25–30 minutes)

Play the Week 2 video segment on the DVD. Invite participants to complete the Video Viewer Guide for Week 2 in the participant workbook as they watch (page 67).

Group Discussion (20–35 minutes, depending on session length)

Note: More material is provided than you will have time to include. Before the session, select what you want to cover.

Video Discussion Questions

- Think about a season of waiting you experienced. What was it like?
- What provisions of God have you taken for granted before? When has your lack of gratitude led to grumbling or complaining, and what effect did that have on you and others?
- In a relationship with God, how are love and trust connected? How has your ability to recognize God's love for you affected your ability to trust Him?

God is never late, but sometimes He cuts it really close! Knowing the people's tendency to forget, Samuel set up a reminder for them, placing a remembrance stone between Mizpah and Shen. (Day 1)

- Read 1 Samuel 7:1-12. Why do you think Samuel set up a remembrance stone for the Israelites?
- What are some markers from your story that have been like remembrance stones to remind you of God's movement in your life?

The elders saw a storm coming, so they asked for a king. Why a king and not a judge? Possibly, they had seen in the other nations around them the value of having one united nation led by one king. They might have believed this to be the best thing for the security and survival of their nation. (Day 1)

- Read 1 Samuel 8:1-9. Why did the elders of Israel decide to meet with Samuel? What did they want and why? (page 44)
- If you had been on that elder board, would you have asked for a king? Why or why not?
- Why do you think the Israelites wanted a king?

In their attempt to *gain* control, the Israelites would soon realize they had actually *relinquished* it....Samuel warned them that a king would take not only their money but also their sons for his army and their daughters for workers in his palace....

The power of government will always come at the cost of individual freedom. Yet, often in its absence there is anarchy. The trick is finding the perfect balance between the two in order to provide for national security and the people's well-being. (Day 2)

- Read 1 Samuel 8:19-22. What does God tell Samuel in verse 22? (page 47)
- Has God ever given you something you asked for and it turned out differently than you expected? Explain.

If the elders had gone throughout the land looking for a king, they would have found no one better than Saul, according to earthly standards. They would have chosen him themselves. God knew what they wanted, and He gave it to them. No fanfare required. (Day 2)

- Read 1 Samuel 9:1-2. What are the attributes of Saul? (page 47) Do you think appearance matters in a leader? Explain.
- Read 1 Samuel 16:7. What does this verse say about outer appearance? (page 47)
- In what ways does our outer appearance speak truth about us? In what ways is it an attempt to cover up our insecurities? (see page 48 for reference)

Like Saul, we go about our lives searching for what we think is lost, when all along it is we who are lost. Through God's divine providence, He directs our steps to some "prophet" who speaks life changing words to us. (Day 3)

- Read 1 Samuel 9:19. Who in your life has acted as a prophet, telling you "all that is in your heart" (NIV)?
- Take a moment to look back at your journey to salvation. Which people did God use to influence you and to draw you to Himself? (page 53)

The real problem in Israel was not that they didn't have a king to lead and protect them. The real problem was that they weren't following the one they had—God. They wanted to plot their own course and secure their own future. Their own desired outcome! They wanted to be like the other nations. They sought after the false power and security the world has to offer. They wanted to make a name for themselves. Had they forgotten the story of Babel? Have we? (Day 3)

- Read 1 Samuel 10:21-24. Where was Saul when his name was announced? Why do you think he might have been there? (page 56)
- How is God calling you to step up to the plate right now? What baggage of life are you hiding behind? Are you feeling ill-equipped? Unprepared? Why? (page 56)

Listen, when you put yourself out there, when you risk being real and vulnerable, when you try to make a difference and influence others, you will always have some group of people who have something negative to say about you. I love what Brené Brown says, "If you're not in the arena also getting your [butt] kicked, I'm not interested in your feedback."[1] Listen, it's easy for others to criticize from the couch! (Day 4)

- Read 1 Samuel 10:25-27. What happened after Saul was declared king? (page 57)
- If you were Saul, how would you have responded to that kind of welcome? What do you think you risk by putting yourself out there in a leadership role?
- Can you share about a time you took a risk and put your real self out there? Were you accepted, or did you take some heat? Explain.

Wow, the people of Jabesh-gilead (who were Israelites) found themselves between a real rock and a hard place. Talk about a lose-lose situation. Obviously, they did not believe that if they fought the Ammonites they would prove victorious. Therefore, they offered to surrender and become their slaves. How sad, considering that four hundred years before God had freed Israel from bondage under the Egyptians. He had established them as a free nation! Yet now a part of this nation is once again facing bondage. (Day 4)

- Read 1 Samuel 11:1-2. What was the situation that Jabesh-gilead found themselves in? What condition for a covenant did Nahash require? Why? (page 59)
- Do you see any similarities between Nahash and our enemy, Satan? (page 60)
- Has the enemy ever discouraged you from taking a leadership role? Explain.

If we do not recognize our patterns and do the healing work, a new king, new job, new marriage, or new town will not prevent us from repeating them. (Day 5)

- Read 1 Samuel 12:6-15. What was Samuel's point? Why was Samuel making this case? (page 65)
- What pattern were the Israelites repeating?
- How have you repeated sinful patterns in your own life? What was the result?

---

1 Brené Brown, "Why Your Critics Aren't the Ones Who Count," 99U, December 4, 2013, YouTube video, 8:53, https://www.youtube.com/watch?v=8-JXOnFOXQk.

Deeper Conversation (15 minutes)

Divide into smaller groups of two or three for deeper conversation. (Encourage the women to break into different groups each week.) If you'd like, before the session, write on a dry erase board or chart paper the question(s) you want the groups to discuss. You could also do this in the form of a handout. Give a two-minute warning before time is up so the groups can wrap up their discussions.

- Revisit the Prayer Prompt for Day 4 (page 62) and discuss the ways in which God is asking you to make a difference.

    ◊ Where is God calling you to show compassion or create opportunities for folks who are struggling?
    ◊ What blessings are in the forefront of your awareness, and how can you share those blessings?
    ◊ What story of brokenness could you share with those who might need to hear it?

Closing Prayer (3–5 minutes)

Close the session by taking personal prayer requests from group members and leading the group in prayer. Encourage members to participate by praying out loud for one another and the requests given (as they are comfortable doing so).

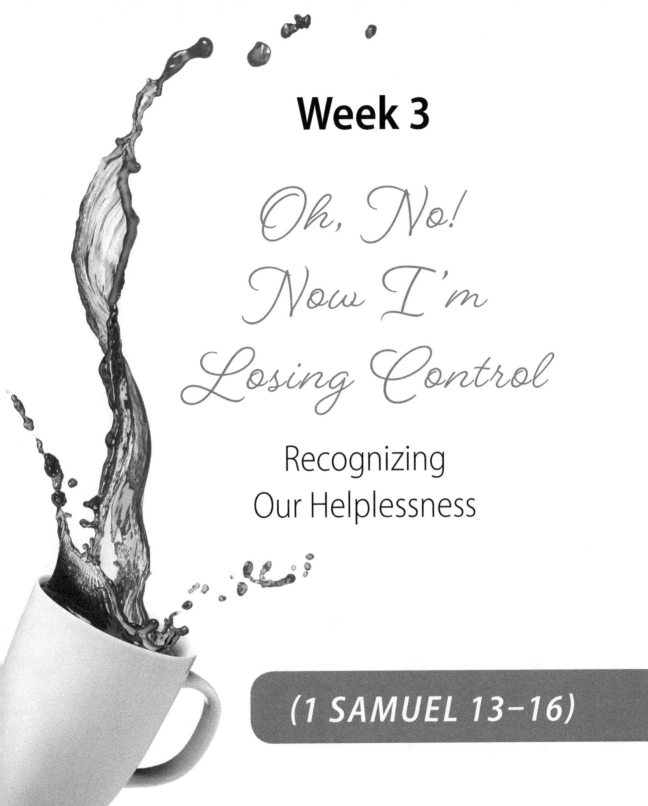

Week 3

Oh, No! Now I'm Losing Control

Recognizing Our Helplessness

(1 SAMUEL 13–16)

Leader Prep (Before the Session)

Overview

This week we followed Saul and Samuel into battle—with each other and into an actual battle. Ultimately Samuel prophesies that Saul's kingship is over and that he is to be replaced with "a man after [God's] own heart" (1 Samuel 13:14). This does not sit well with Saul, and he presses on into battle against the Philistines. We see Saul becoming more anxious and fearful and grasping for control when God is asking for a surrendered heart.

In this session, we'll explore our own tendencies to grasp for control when God is asking us to surrender.

Key Scriptures

13-14a*"That was a fool thing to do," Samuel said to Saul. "If you had kept the appointment that your God commanded, by now God would have set a firm and lasting foundation under your kingly rule over Israel. As it is, your kingly rule is already falling to pieces. God is out looking for your replacement right now."*

(1 Samuel 13:13-14a MSG)

23*Search me, O God, and know my heart!*
 Try me and know my thoughts!
24*And see if there be any grievous way in me,*
 and lead me in the way everlasting!
 (Psalm 139:23-24)

4*For everything that was written in the past was written to teach us, so that through the endurance taught in the Scriptures and the encouragement they provide we might have hope.*

5May the God who gives endurance and encouragement give you the same attitude of mind toward each other that Christ Jesus had, 6so that with one mind and one voice you may glorify the God and Father of our Lord Jesus Christ.

(Romans 15:4-6 NIV)

The Lord is not slow to fulfill his promise as some count slowness, but is patient toward you, not wishing that any should perish, but that all should reach repentance.

(2 Peter 3:9)

What You Will Need

- *Lose Control* DVD (or downloads) and a DVD player or computer
- Bible and *Lose Control* participant workbook for reference
- Dry erase board or chart paper and markers (optional)
- Stick-on nametags and markers (optional)
- iPod, smartphone, or tablet and portable speaker (optional)

Session Outline

Welcome and Opening Prayer (2 minutes)

In order to create a warm, welcoming environment as the women are gathering before the session begins, consider lighting one or more candles, providing coffee or other refreshments, and/or playing worship music. (Bring an iPod, smartphone, or tablet and a portable speaker if desired.) Be sure to provide nametags if the women do not know one another or you have new participants in your group. Then, when you are ready to begin, open the group in prayer, or invite someone else to do so.

Icebreaker (3 minutes)

Invite the women to share short responses to the following question:

- Do you find it easy or difficult to ask for help? Why?

Video (25–30 minutes)

Play the Week 3 video segment on the DVD. Invite participants to complete the Video Viewer Guide for Week 3 in the participant workbook as they watch (page 101).

Group Discussion (20–35 minutes, depending on session length)

Note: More material is provided than you will have time to include. Before the session, select what you want to cover.

Video Discussion Questions

- How have Jesus's words brought you peace?
- How have Jesus's words set you free?
- How have Jesus's words brought you restoration or new life?
- Whose words have been carrying more weight: what culture says about you, what someone else says about you, what you say about you, or what God says about you?

Participant Workbook Discussion Questions

> It doesn't take a brain surgeon to know that the only one who can control creation is the One who created it. (Day 1)

- Read 1 Samuel 12:16-18. In order to get the people's attention, what did Samuel ask of the Lord? (page 70)
- What has God done in your life to get your attention?

> Navigating this world takes endurance and, most of all, encouragement from others who have experienced similar struggles. Our hope is not found in our accomplishments but in Jesus Christ, who accomplished our salvation on the cross. He is our living hope. This is the encouragement of the Scriptures, and this is the encouragement we are to share with the world around us—all doing our part to become a choir with many voices and many stories, all harmonizing together to glorify the Lord Jesus Christ. (Day 1)

- Read Romans 15:4-6. What do these verses tell us about God's desire for us? (page 71)
- What kinds of situations have built up endurance in your life?
- Why is it so powerful for believers to share their struggles with one another?

> With the weight of the nation on his shoulders and facing an impossible situation, Saul had made the choice to proceed to war without Samuel. (Day 2)

- Read 1 Samuel 13:11-12. What would you have done in that situation? Describe a time in your life when you felt incredible pressure to make a decision. What was the outcome? (page 77)
- Read 1 Samuel 13:13-14. Do you ever hear words of disappointment from the past ringing in your head—possibly from someone you admired? If so, describe how they make you feel. (page 78)
- Are there still times when you are subconsciously trying to prove those words wrong? Explain. (page 78)

> God is a God of freedom! Failing to recognize this was often the problem in ancient times, and it's often the problem today. Why do we have all of the rules we have? Are we attempting to control the flesh with outward obedience, or are we allowing God to come in and change the heart? Isn't obedience actually motivated by love? (Day 3)

- Review the details of 1 Samuel 14 together. What do you think Saul was trying to prove with his actions in this chapter, and to whom was he trying to prove it? What core feelings or fears do you think were going on in Saul that produced these reactionary behaviors? (page 84)
- What happens to *you* when you worry about what other people think? (page 84)
- How might this people-pleasing breed fear of failure? How is the fear of failure connected to the fear of losing control? (pages 84–85)

> [Fear] can make us apprehensive and unable to make decisions, and on the other hand, it can make us impulsive with our decisions as we grasp for control. (Day 3)

- What fears might be causing you to be overly passive or overly involved in certain situations? (page 85)
- What are a couple of situations that have exposed your fears? What was the core of each underlying fear? (page 86) How did you walk through those fears?

I have to admit that at times the justice of God is hard for me to accept and understand, but if I am truly honest, His unrelenting mercy is even harder to comprehend. In the end, I choose to trust the discernment of a God who is willing to "blot out" my sins simply based upon my faith, and who offers that opportunity to *all people*. (Day 4)

- Read the following passages: Psalm 51:1, 9; 2 Peter 3:9; and Ezekiel 33:11. What do these verses tell us about the heart of God? (page 91)
- Compare 1 Samuel 15:3 with 1 Samuel 15:9. In what way did Saul disobey the command of God? According to 1 Samuel 15:11, what was God's response? (pages 91–92)
- Read 1 Samuel 15:17-21. How did Saul respond to the accusations of Samuel? (page 94) Would you say Saul is surrendered to God or grasping for his own control? Why?
- If God is generous with mercy, why do you think we are often resistant to coming clean with our sin and rebellion? What does it mean to choose surrender over control?

The word of tension between Samuel and Saul had made its way throughout the land. Samuel's fear caused him anxiety, and this anxiety drove his need for control and certainty. Instead of trusting God for each step, he wanted a blueprint laid out. God graciously gave the old prophet added information. Remember, even great men and women of God can have moments of fear. (Day 5)

- Read 1 Samuel 16:1-3. What did God tell Samuel to do once he arrived at the home of Jesse? (page 98)
- Read Zechariah 4:6. How would you explain this verse in your own words? (page 99)
- How does Zechariah 4:6 speak to God's choice of David as a king?

Deeper Conversation (15 minutes)

Divide into smaller groups of two or three for deeper conversation. (Encourage the women to break into different groups each week.) If you'd like, before the session, write on a dry erase board or chart paper the question(s) you want the groups to discuss. You could also do this in the form of a handout. Give a two-minute warning before time is up so the groups can wrap up their discussions.

- Read Psalm 51:7-8. In what ways do you need the Lord's restoration in your life? (page 97)
- How has fear of failure crippled you in the past?
- What might God be asking you to do that scares you?

Closing Prayer (3–5 minutes, depending on session length)

Close the session by taking personal prayer requests from group members and leading the group in prayer. Encourage members to participate by praying out loud for one another and the requests given (as they are comfortable doing so).

Week 4

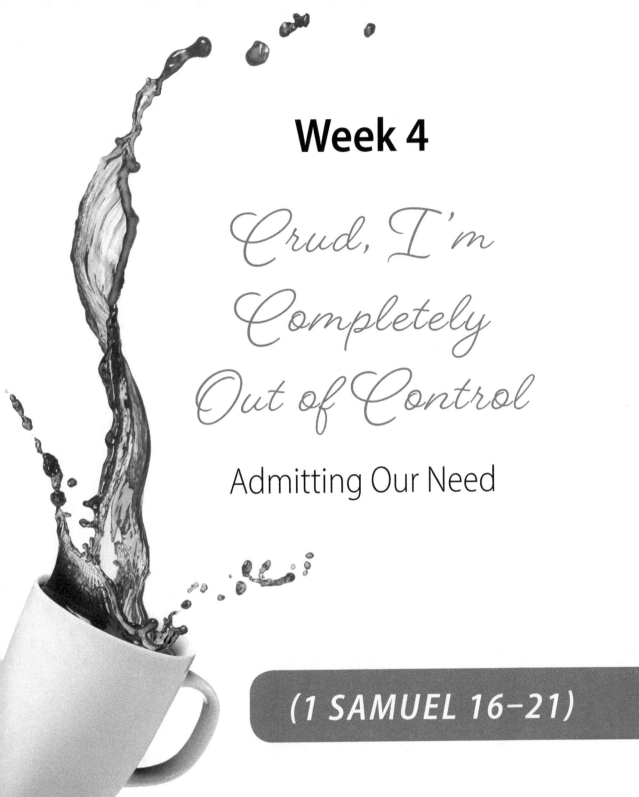

Crud, I'm Completely Out of Control

Admitting Our Need

(1 SAMUEL 16–21)

Leader Prep (Before the Session)

Overview

This week we definitely saw the wheels come off in both Saul's and David's lives. We explored God's sovereignty, which led to questions like, "Does God's sovereignty make Him the agent of delivery for bad events?" We answered that question by discovering that God doesn't magically remove our pain but allows our pain to be our teacher.

As we read the story of David and Goliath, we explored the bullies and giants in our lives today and how we might already have the unique-to-us tools to take them down. We also explored friendship and the beauty of covenant, and we ended our week remembering our identity and our mission.

Key Scriptures

¹³*When tempted, no one should say, "God is tempting me." For God cannot be tempted by evil, nor does he tempt anyone;* ¹⁴*but each person is tempted when they are dragged away by their own evil desire and enticed.*

(James 1:13-14 NIV)

In this is love, not that we have loved God but that he loved us and sent his Son to be the propitiation for our sins.

(1 John 4:10)

^{5b}*"I will never leave you nor forsake you."* ⁶*So we can confidently say,*

> *"The Lord is my helper;*
> *I will not fear;*
> *what can man do to me?"*

(Hebrews 13:5b-6)

[1]*With my voice I cry out to the* LORD;
 with my voice I plead for mercy to the LORD.
[2]*I pour out my complaint before him;*
 I tell my trouble before him.

(Psalm 142:1-2)

What You Will Need

- *Lose Control* DVD (or downloads) and a DVD player or computer
- Bible and *Lose Control* participant workbook for reference
- Dry erase board or chart paper and markers (optional)
- Stick-on nametags and markers (optional)
- iPod, smartphone, or tablet and portable speaker (optional)

Session Outline

Welcome and Opening Prayer (2 minutes)

In order to create a warm, welcoming environment as the women are gathering before the session begins, consider lighting one or more candles, providing coffee or other refreshments, and/or playing worship music. (Bring an iPod, smartphone, or tablet and a portable speaker if desired.) Be sure to provide nametags if the women do not know one another or you have new participants in your group. Then, when you are ready to begin, open the group in prayer, or invite someone else to do so.

Icebreaker (3 minutes)

Invite the women to share short responses to the following question:

- What is something someone has said to you in a difficult time that was not helpful?

Video (25–30 minutes)

Play the Week 4 video segment on the DVD. Invite participants to complete the Video Viewer Guide for Week 4 in the participant workbook as they watch (page 135).

Group Discussion (20–35 minutes, depending on session length)

Note: More material is provided than you will have time to include. Before the session, select what you want to cover.

Video Discussion Questions

- Have you ever been afraid of something, only to learn there was no real reason to be afraid?
- What are some "cookie jar" experiences that give you confidence in what God is asking of you now?
- How has God uniquely equipped you for situations you're facing right now?

Participant Workbook Discussion Questions

> God had empowered Saul to see and do things he normally would not be able to do. He had given Saul a calling and a purpose, which comes with responsibility. If Saul were unwilling to obey the commands of God, then God would choose another.
>
> We can track with that. But what do we make of the second part of the verse: "A harmful spirit from the LORD tormented him"? The word *torment* here is *ba'ath*, which means "to fall upon, startle, terrify."[1] (Day 1)

- Read 1 Samuel 16:14. What questions does this verse raise for you?
- Read James 1:13; 1 John 1:5; and 1 Corinthians 14:33. How would you summarize these verses, especially as they relate to evil? (page 104)
- If God won't tempt someone to do evil, would He send an evil spirit to torment a person? Can the author of peace send confusion? Share your thoughts about how we might reconcile the New Testament Scriptures (above) with the Old Testament examples of Genesis 30 and 1 Samuel 2:6. (page 105)
- Read Proverbs 1:23-33. In light of this proverb, what was Saul's responsibility for his own situation? (page 105)

> God sent the future king to soothe the reigning one. David was not there to threaten but to soothe. The Hebrew word for *soothe*

1. Strong's Concordance, s.v. "ba'ath," Blue Letter Bible, https://www.blueletterbible.org/lang/lexicon/lexicon.cfm?Strongs=H1204&t=KJV.

is *ravach*, and it means to be wide or spacious, to breathe easily, or to be relieved.[2] In other words, when the walls were caving in on Saul, David brought the open space and peace of the pasture. David's music allowed Saul to breathe!

Music is an amazing thing, isn't it? (Day 1)

- Read 1 Samuel 16:15-23. What solution did Saul's servants suggest for his mental anguish? Who is named in verse 18, and how is he described? (page 106)
- Read Job 38:4-7 and Revelation 5:8-10. What role does music play in each passage? What seems to be its purpose? (page 107)
- How has music soothed your anxieties?
- What is your favorite song to sing *to* God? What is your favorite song to sing *about* God?

We all face giants, those bullies who strike fear in our hearts. Maybe it's a person, a pressure, or a worry, but we all face some kind of giant. (Day 2)

- Review the story of David and Goliath in 1 Samuel 17. How might David have felt seeing Goliath for the first time?
- Which giants have taunted you in the past? (refer to page 110)
- What do you think this statement means: "Fear causes us to lose perspective. It is the great exaggerator"?
- Have you allowed fear to magnify your situation, convincing you that victory is impossible? Are you attempting to fight your giant in your own strength or in God's strength? (page 113)

David could not go into battle with someone else's armor. It wasn't his "cookie jar"!

Friend, there is only one you. No one else has the beautiful combination of gifts and talents that you do. No one else has the upbringing you do—all the events that molded you into who you are. We all face battles and we all must reach into our own cookie jar for strength.

---

2 Strong's Concordance, s.v. "ravach," Blue Letter Bible, https://www.blueletterbible.org/lang/lexicon/lexicon.cfm?t=kjv&strongs=h7304.

> There is not a battle that God has called you to face that He has not also equipped you to win. (Day 3)

- Read 1 Samuel 17:38-39. Has there been a time in your life when you had the armor but not the heart? What good was the armor to you in that situation? (page 117)
- What are some of the events that have molded you into who you are? How did they make you feel? What did you learn or how did you grow? (page 117)

> I believe [David and Jonathan's friendship] is the most beautiful and vulnerable picture of true friendship in Scripture. Jonathan removed his robe, tunic, and weapons, which *symbolized* his position as the crown prince of Israel, and gave them to David. The one who had the royal right to the throne *sacrificed* himself and his position for his friend. Then he *pledged* his allegiance to David, putting his own life on the line for his friend. And the motivation for it all? Love! (Day 4)

- Read John 15:13. What is the greatest expression of love? (page 122)
- Read Deuteronomy 7:6-9. What was the motivation behind the covenant with Abraham? (page 122)
- Read 1 John 4:10. What was God's motivation in sending Jesus? (page 122)
- How would you define friendship? How have you sacrificed for your friends? How has a friend sacrificed out of love for you?

> Along the way, [Saul] forgot he was on a mission. He was anointed to lead the people of Israel according to the purposes of God. Yet, instead of keeping his eyes on God and his mission, he allowed the pains, pressures, and comparisons of this world to turn his mission into his identity. (Day 4)

- Read 1 Samuel 18:6-9. What happened that turned Saul's envy into jealousy? (page 124) What is the difference between envy and jealousy?
- If someone asked you to describe yourself, what would you say? In other words, who are you? (page 125)
- What is the difference between what you *do* and who you *are*?
- How is our mission related to our identity?

> David became the man after God's own heart in the shepherd's field,
> but it would take the wilderness to prepare him to be king. (Day 5)

- Review the timeline of events as David's comforts are removed in 1 Samuel 19–21. What was taken away from David? (see pages 128, 129, 131)
- How do difficult events in our lives prepare us for future situations? Share an example from your own life.

> When our eyes betray us, our faith believes in what we cannot see.
> (Day 5)

- Read Hebrews 13:5b-6. How do these verses apply to our study this week?
- Read Psalm 142:1-2. When have you pleaded for mercy and poured out your complaints to God? How was God faithful to you?

Deeper Conversation (15 minutes)

Divide into smaller groups of two or three for deeper conversation. (Encourage the women to break into different groups each week.) If you'd like, before the session, write on a dry erase board or chart paper the question(s) you want the groups to discuss. You could also do this in the form of a handout. Give a two-minute warning before time is up so the groups can wrap up their discussions.

- Recall your time with God using the Prayer Prompt for Day 5 (page 134). What did God bring to mind about what you once may have counted as loss but now see the beauty and growth that came from it?
- If you are currently in a time of loss, share your heart with your sisters sitting next to you and let them pray for you and speak words of life into your heart.
- What do you think Mary Shannon meant by the statement, "God is not in the business of magically removing our pain, but He will allow pain to be our teacher"? How has this been true in your life?

Closing Prayer (3–5 minutes, depending on session length)

Close the session by taking personal prayer requests from group members and leading the group in prayer. Encourage members to participate by praying out loud for one another and the requests given (as they are comfortable doing so).

Week 5

Control?
Over What?

Acknowledging
We Can't Control
Anything But Ourselves

(1 SAMUEL 22–26)

Leader Prep (Before the Session)

Overview

This week had no shortage of action and drama. We watched David go from hiding in a cave to calling Saul to task. We also saw Samuel pass away and a national funeral that David didn't get to attend. We read about a lot of out-of-control-ness this week, but we also saw David call to mind the goodness and faithfulness of God.

Key Scriptures

"For I know the plans I have for you, declares the LORD, plans for welfare and not for evil, to give you a future and a hope."

(Jeremiah 29:11)

And we know that for those who love God all things work together for good, for those who are called according to his purpose.

(Romans 8:28)

"For whoever wants to save their life will lose it, but whoever loses their life for me will find it."
(Matthew 16:25 NIV)

[18-20]*My dear children, let's not just talk about love; let's practice real love. This is the only way we'll know we're living truly, living in God's reality. It's also the way to shut down debilitating self-criticism, even when there is something to it. For God is greater than our worried hearts and knows more about us than we do ourselves.*

(1 John 3:18-20 MSG)

What You Will Need

- *Lose Control* DVD (or downloads) and a DVD player or computer
- Bible and *Lose Control* participant workbook for reference
- Dry erase board or chart paper and markers (optional)

- Stick-on nametags and markers (optional)
- iPod, smartphone, or tablet and portable speaker (optional)

Session Outline

Welcome and Opening Prayer (2 minutes)

In order to create a warm, welcoming environment as the women are gathering before the session begins, consider lighting one or more candles, providing coffee or other refreshments, and/or playing worship music. (Bring an iPod, smartphone, or tablet and a portable speaker if desired.) Be sure to provide nametags if the women do not know one another or you have new participants in your group. Then, when you are ready to begin, open the group in prayer, or invite someone else to do so.

Icebreaker (3 minutes)

Invite the women to share short responses to the following question:

- When have the wheels come off in your life in a "so-crazy-it's-funny" kind of way? For example—spilling your coffee while commuting, then getting a flat tire, then being late for a meeting, and so forth.

Video (25–30 minutes)

Play the Week 5 video segment on the DVD. Invite participants to complete the Video Viewer Guide for Week 5 in the participant workbook as they watch (page 167).

Group Discussion (20–35 minutes, depending on session length)

Note: More material is provided than you will have time to include. Before the session, select what you want to cover.

Video Discussion Questions

- Have you ever tried to run from your pain? What happened? Which of the biblical characters mentioned in the video who endured pain, other than David and Saul, do you resonate with the most? Why? (Abraham, Jacob, Joseph, Moses, Peter, Paul, Jesus)

- How has God used your brokenness to help someone else?

Participant Workbook Discussion Questions

When the wheels of life are coming off and we have no control, we are forced to face our true beliefs about God. Is He in control? Does He truly love me? Is He good? How can a good God allow so much pain? (Day 1)

- Read 1 Samuel 21:10-15. Where did David choose to flee [and why was he on the run]? What did David do once he realized he had been recognized, and why? (page 137)
- Have you ever tried to get away from or hide from God? How did that go?
- Read Psalm 142:4. Have you had questions like David was wrestling with? Have you ever felt like this? Have you ever thought to yourself "no one cares for my soul"? (page 139)

We will never understand some events this side of eternity. Why do bad things happen to good people? What things have been foreseen by God that will play out in our present-day lives by our own and others' free will? These thoughts are too much for me to grasp. When I cannot fathom what God is doing in the midst of what is happening, I choose to rely on His goodness. (Day 1)

- Read Jeremiah 29:11 and Romans 8:28. What assurance do these verses give us? (page 140)
- Read Hebrews 12:1-2. How do you feel knowing that you are surrounded by a "cloud of witnesses"? (page 141)

No matter how much we may want to stay in the cave, life has a way of moving on, and so must we. The cave is a place to reroute, not a place to relocate. There is one thing I have learned from being in the cave: you truly find out who your people are! (Day 2)

- Read 1 Samuel 22:2. Who made up the motley crew that accumulate in the cave with David? (page 142)
- Why do "cave seasons" show us who "our people" are? How has that been true in your own life?

How often in real life do we analyze our circumstances in an attempt to understand God? When bad things happen, we say, "Why is God doing this to me?" When good things happen, we say, "Thank you, God, for coming through." When Pharaoh let the people go, they rejoiced at what God had done. Yet, at the edge of the Red Sea, they accused Him of sending them out into the desert to die. We are so shortsighted. (Day 2)

- Read Proverbs 12:15; Philippians 4:8; James 1:2-3; and Philippians 4:19. What insights bubbled up for you as you meditated and studied on these verses? (see pages 145–146)
- Read 1 Samuel 23:9-14. What did David do when he got wind of Saul's plan? (page 146)
- How did David lean into God's reality instead of perception?

Personally, I feel so much closer to God when I am out in His beautiful creation. When I am sitting on the top of a mountain looking out at the vast desert below and the many mountain ranges in the distance, I am reminded of the enormity of my God. He is powerful, creative, and beautiful. When up there, the world's problems seem much smaller in comparison. You don't have to be an extreme outdoors person to experience this. Go to the park or anywhere you can put your feet in some grass and see a beautiful tree waving in the wind. (Day 3)

- Recall a time when you were able to go outside and spend time meditating on God or Scripture, breathing in deeply, and syncing your soul to the rhythms of creation. How did it help you to feel closer to God? (page 151)
- Read Psalm 63. What key words and phrases reflect the environment around David? (pages 149)
- How does being out in God's beautiful creation change your perspective on control?

When you are on the outside, all sorts of questions plague your mind. *Does anyone miss me? Do they ever think of me? What do they think of me? Was every gesture of affection genuine?* When you are the one on the outside, insecurity has a way of making everything seem to be about you. Rejection hurts, and it can fuel powerful anger if you are not careful. (Day 4)

- Read 1 Samuel 25:1. What national event was happening in Israel? How do you think David was feeling upon receiving the news about Samuel? (page 154)
- Why wasn't David able to be at the funeral?
- Describe a time when you felt rejected or left out. What thoughts and emotions did you experience? How did you heal—or have you? (page 155)

David refused to give in to violence in order to free himself of pain. By doing so, we see that David was willing to sit in the pain and wait for God to move. To be honest, living with the pain is so hard for me. When I am sad and heartbroken, I honestly want to do anything to make it stop. (Day 5)

- Read 1 Samuel 26:1-12. Why did David refuse to lay a hand on Saul? What items did David take? (page 162)
- Have you ever made a choice you regret because you just wanted to stop the pain? Have you ever forfeited growth for comfort? Has there been a time in your life when you wish you would have sat a little longer in the pain and discomfort before making a decision? Has there been a time when sitting in the pain was your only choice? Explain. (page 162)

Sometimes we may think we have gone too far to turn back. We won't risk humiliation to find restoration. We won't risk being wrong to find unity. We won't risk swallowing our pride to find help. We believe too much damage has been done. But that is not true! It is never too late to do the right thing. (Day 5)

- Read 1 Samuel 26:13-25. What is going on in these verses? (refer to pages 163–165)
- Read Proverbs 3:3. How does this proverb apply to Samuel and Saul in this point in their story?
- Read 1 John 3:18-20. How would you describe the difference between talking about love and practicing love? (page 164)

- When was the last time you made a decision because it was the right thing to do? How hard was it to stick to what you had decided when all of the fear and heartache came flooding in? Did you stick to it? Describe the situation. (page 165)

Deeper Conversation (15 minutes)

Divide into smaller groups of two or three for deeper conversation. (Encourage the women to break into different groups each week.) If you'd like, before the session, write on a dry erase board or chart paper the question(s) you want the groups to discuss. You could also do this in the form of a handout. Give a two-minute warning before time is up so the groups can wrap up their discussions.

> [God] loves you as you are—whether you have praises on your lips or bitterness in your bones. You can trust Him with either, even when life seems completely out of control. Because even then, God is never out of control. (Day 3)

- Would you say you have more praises or bitterness these days? What is causing your praise? What is causing bitterness in your bones?
- What are some spiritual practices that have helped you choose praise over bitterness?

Closing Prayer (3–5 minutes, depending on session length)

Close the session by taking personal prayer requests from group members and leading the group in prayer. Encourage members to participate by praying out loud for one another and the requests given (as they are comfortable doing so).

Week 6

God Really Is in Control

Coming Full Circle to True Belief and Surrender

(1 SAMUEL 27–31)

Leader Prep (Before the Session)

Overview

This week as we've wrapped up our study, we have seen what it looks like to come full circle to true belief and surrender. We learned that we may not have it all together. David certainly didn't. But when we lose control, we can follow David's example and turn our eyes to God, for He is our greatest hope. Whatever detours we have taken, Jesus is the gate back to the right path.

Like David, we must learn to lament our losses, trusting in God's love and provision and believing that His good plans will prevail. Remember, David began as an overlooked son in a shepherd's field, but soon after his anointing he began one massive victory tour. Yet when the tour came to an end, David experienced one loss after another. He lost his family, his home, his best friend, and his mentor, Samuel. He experienced rejection, false accusation, and solitude. For years he lived as a fugitive while holding on to a promise that seemed like a mist. David was forced to live by faith, looking forward without any assurances, while we have the scriptural hindsight to know that God was in control of David's life and destiny. David went on to become the reigning king of Israel, and not only that, but God's own Son came through David's line!

Key Scriptures

David was greatly distressed because the men were talking of stoning him; each one was bitter in spirit because of his sons and daughters. But David found strength in the LORD his God.

(1 Samuel 30:6 NIV)

"Therefore, I tell you, her many sins have been forgiven—as her great love has shown. But whoever has been forgiven little loves little."

(Luke 7:47 NIV)

What You Will Need

- *Lose Control* DVD (or downloads) and a DVD player or computer
- Bible and *Lose Control* participant workbook for reference
- Dry erase board or chart paper and markers (optional)
- Stick-on nametags and markers (optional)
- iPod, smartphone, or tablet and portable speaker (optional)

Session Outline

Welcome and Opening Prayer (2 minutes)

In order to create a warm, welcoming environment as the women are gathering before the session begins, consider lighting one or more candles, providing coffee or other refreshments, and/or playing worship music. (Bring an iPod, smartphone, or tablet and a portable speaker if desired.) Be sure to provide nametags if the women do not know one another or you have new participants in your group. Then, when you are ready to begin, open the group in prayer, or invite someone else to do so.

Icebreaker (3 minutes)

Invite the women to share short responses to the following question:

- When you were a child, what did you want to be when you grew up?

Video (25–30 minutes)

Play the Week 6 video segment on the DVD. Invite participants to complete the Video Viewer Guide for Week 6 in the participant workbook as they watch (page 200).

Group Discussion (20–35 minutes, depending on session length)

Note: More material is provided than you will have time to include. Before the session, select what you want to cover.

Video Discussion Questions

- How do you think hopelessness and helplessness are connected?

- Have you ever tried to control a person or a situation? How did it go awry?
- Have you ever looked at your life and gotten stuck in one scene? What overarching story is God trying to tell with your life?

Participant Workbook Discussion Questions

> Have you ever come to a place in your life where you are willing to settle? After years of battling, you are convinced that the things you once dreamed of either don't exist or they don't exist for *you*. You've tried to be obedient and strong, but nothing ever seems to work out. You concede that you are destined to repeat the same old patterns. So you push those dreams aside and move to the land of "settle" because you need to be seen, to be heard, and to belong. (Day 1)

- When you have lost control, what dreams have you given up and what "lands" have you settled in? (page 170)
- Review the story of Leah in Genesis 29. In what way did Leah have to settle, and why? (page 170)
- How is Leah's story an illustration of giving up control and surrendering to God's plans?

> God sees *you*. You are enough. God hears you, and He understands what you are going through. (Day 1)

- Do you believe that statement? What gives you confidence in those words? If you struggle to believe it, what hinders your confidence in those promises?
- Do you feel like you have to hide your true self from God? Why or why not?

> David was a really good actor!...David was amazing at painting whatever image of himself he needed to survive. One probably gets really good at this when running for one's life.
>
> What about you? Are you good at presenting whatever image you need in order to survive or achieve? Listen, I don't blame anyone for that. I am the best at it! Fear causes us to protect our vulnerable selves. From childhood, we learn how to protect ourselves in whatever environment we grow up in. We read our environment and then we learn to adjust and maneuver for acceptance and love. (Day 2)

- Consider the question: Do others know the real me? Why or why not? Share your reflections. (page 176)
- Ask yourself: Do *I* know the real me, or do I just see myself through other people's filters? Share your reflections. (page 176)
- How do you try to protect yourself in a scary or unknown situation with other people?

We can have the best intentions. We can make the best decisions we can based on the information we have. We can be convinced in our hearts that we are on the right path doing God's will, yet we can still end up in a place of defeat. At first we grieve, and then we may blame others or ourselves. We analyze every step that got us to this place. We play the *shoulda, woulda, coulda* game. But eventually we must come to a place of being alone with God, shutting down all the other voices in our lives, and asking Him, "Where do I go from here?" (Day 2)

- Have you ever felt attacked on multiple sides? How did you react? (page 180)
- Read 1 Samuel 30:6. What did David do, according to this verse? (page 179) What does it mean to strengthen yourself in the Lord?
- Have you ever played the game of *shoulda, woulda, coulda*? What happened in the end?

Living by sight is one of the earliest tactics of the enemy of our souls. Oh, the gateway of the eye. (Day 3)

- Read Genesis 3:6. What did the woman see and why did she think it was good?
- When has what you *saw* made you question God's goodness or faithfulness? (page 182)

As we've seen throughout our study, fear is the root of all control issues. Fear of the unknown, fear of failure, fear of success, fear of change, fear of isolation, and fear of what others think. The more we fear, the more we try to control. The problem is that we do not have the power to control most things. We cannot control others and we cannot control outcomes. The only thing we can control is ourselves, and sometimes even that seems impossible. (Day 4)

- Now that we are near the end of our study, consider what insights or clarity you have received regarding your fears. What are you afraid of? What or whom are you trying to control? (page 190)
- What have you learned in this study about the connection between your fears and your need for control?
- What might have happened in Saul's life if he had been able to bring some humility and vulnerability to the table?

> God is calling us to allow Him to show us our hidden places.... To allow Him to heal us and replace whatever lie is hidden there with His truth.
>
> Fear is what grows out of a lie. As we've seen throughout our study, digging down through the layers of our fears helps us determine the lies beneath. (Day 4)

- Read 2 Samuel 1:15-16. What action did David take, and why? (page 192)
- What are some "spies" that try to sabotage the truth in your life? How can you eliminate them?
- As you consider the story of Samuel, Saul, and David, think about trusting God in the hidden places in our hearts. What have *you* discovered about your need for God to work even in those shadowy, hidden places?

> To lose control—to surrender our lives to Jesus—is how we find our soul. (Day 5)

- Read 2 Samuel 1:19-26. What all was David grieving in these verses? (page 198)
- After all that he had endured under the hand of Saul, why do you think David was able to write such a heartfelt lament for him?
- Read Luke 7:47. What promise does this tell us about God's forgiveness?
- How do we find our souls when we lose control?

Deeper Conversation (15 minutes)

Divide into smaller groups of two or three for deeper conversation. If you'd like, before the session, write on a dry erase board or chart paper the question(s) you want the groups to discuss. You could also do this in the form of a handout. Give a two-minute warning before time is up so the groups can wrap up their discussions.

- Reflect on the Prayer Prompt from Day 5 and discuss what God brought to mind. What is keeping you from coming to the party and taking your seat at the table? What is holding you back? Are you living as a fearful slave or a beloved daughter? Explain. (page 199)
- How have you known the extravagant love of God to be faithful and a sure foundation, even as you might be losing control?

Closing Prayer (3–5 minutes, depending on session length)

Close the session by taking personal prayer requests from group members and leading the group in prayer. Encourage members to participate by praying out loud for one another and the requests given (as they are comfortable doing so).

Video Viewer Guide Answers

Week 1
work / control
do / Jesus
insecurities
love cup
Feelings / slaves
equipped
His

Week 2
delays / detours
model / endorse
trust
Awareness
represent
Spirit / idol
love

Week 3
peace
captives free
restore
bring life
define / develop
lasting effect
Word

Week 4
anticipation / reality
perspective / sight
cloud / rain
face / bullies
equipped
armor

Week 5
question
sorrows / human
Nothing
mystery
race / weight
brokenness

Week 6
hopeless
withdraw
response
work
Friday / Sunday
hovering
settle

CPSIA information can be obtained
at www.ICGtesting.com
Printed in the USA
LVHW010836100920
665515LV00003B/3